# Why Is a Guinea Pig Called a Guinea Pig If It Looks Like a Hamster?
## And Other Animals We Confuse!

By Donna and Dr. Delvin Defoe

## Dedication

To our loving son, Justin, whose curiosity about pets and other animals inspired the creation of this book.

Edited by Whitney Hill

Illustrated by Jared Boser

Copyright © 2024 by Donna Defoe and Dr. Delvin Defoe

All rights reserved. No portion of this book may be reproduced in any form without prior permission from the copyright owner of this book.

ISBN: 979-8-9915139-0-6

## Contents

**Animals We Confuse** .................................................. 4
**Pigs** .......................................................................... 5
**Guinea Pigs and Hamsters** ..................................... 6
**Crocodiles and Alligators** ..................................... 12
**Toads and Frogs** ................................................... 18
**Porpoises and Dolphins** ........................................ 24
**Emus and Ostriches** .............................................. 30
**Back to Our Questions!** ........................................ 36
**What Did We Learn?** ............................................. 38

Have you ever wondered why a guinea pig is called a "pig" if it looks so much like a hamster?

Or if crocodiles and alligators eat the same things?

Or if the hopping creature in your backyard is really a toad or a frog?

Let's explore together the differences between these and other easily confused creatures!

## But first, let's learn a bit about pigs!

Pigs have large heads and long snouts. They are pink in color and have short stiff hair.

Other types of pigs have different hair textures and colors, but all pigs look very similar.

**Now, let's learn about guinea pigs!**

# Why is a guinea pig called a guinea pig if it looks like a hamster?

Do guinea pigs look like hamsters?

Which one is a guinea pig, and which one is a hamster?

## Do guinea pigs *really* look like hamsters?

Yes! They are both cute and furry, with pointy noses! As you can see, side by side, they appear to belong to the same animal family—the rodent family.

## Do they live in the same place?
## Do they eat the same kinds of things?

Let's explore the ways guinea pigs and hamsters are alike and the ways in which they are different.

# Guinea Pig Facts

Guinea pigs can live for 4 to 10 years. They originally come from South America, where they live in cooler, grassy regions. The color of their fur can be black, chocolate, red, tan, cream, or white. They are typically between 8 and 12 inches long and weigh between 1½ and 2½ pounds. Guinea pigs like to eat hay, grass, fruits, vegetables, and small clumped-together balls that they produce themselves—in other words, they eat their own poo.

**Does a guinea pig make a good pet? Yes, it does!** It is small and friendly. You can keep it safely in a cage.

# Hamster Facts

Hamsters can live for 1½ to 3 years. They originally come from Syria in the Middle East, where they live in places like deserts or grasslands. The color of their fur can be gold, black, cream, orange, white, rust, or a variety of other colors. They typically grow up to 7 inches in length and weigh between 3 and 7 ounces. Hamsters like to eat seeds, nuts, fruits, vegetables, insects, and worms. They have pouches in their cheeks that can stretch to transport food.

**Does a hamster make a good pet? Yes, it does!** It is small, and you can keep it safely in a cage.

Wow! There are many types of guinea pigs and hamsters from all over the world. We compared the guinea pig, which originated in South America, and the hamster, which originated in Syria. Both animals eat fruits and vegetables, but hamsters eat insects and worms, while guinea pigs eat their own poo. Both animals come in multiple colors. Guinea pigs are bigger than hamsters and live much longer.

**The table below lists the differences between guinea pigs and hamsters:**

|  | Guinea Pig | Hamster |
|---|---|---|
| Place of Origin | South America | Middle East, Syria |
| Habitat | cooler grassy regions, rocky areas | deserts, grasslands |
| Color of Fur | black, chocolate, red, tan, cream, white | gold, black, cream, cinnamon, white, and many more colors |
| Length | 8 to 12 inches (20.3 to 30.5 centimeters) | up to 7 inches (up to 17.8 centimeters) |
| Weight | 1½ to 2½ pounds (0.7 to 1.1 kilograms) | 3 to 7 ounces (85 to 198.5 grams) |
| Food | hay, grass, vitamin C-rich fruits and green vegetables, and their own poo | seeds, nuts, fruits, vegetables, insects, and worms |
| Lifespan | 4 to 10 years | 1½ to 3 years |

Now that we have found our answers, we can't stop there! Let's explore why other animals look alike but are called by different names.

# Why is a crocodile called a crocodile if it looks like an alligator?

**Do crocodiles look like alligators?**

**Which one is the crocodile, and which one is the alligator?**

## Do crocodiles *really* look like alligators?

Yes! They are both scaly, with long sharp teeth.
As you can see, side by side, they look like the same animal. They share the same ancestor. Both are large reptiles that can live in water and on land.

## In what other ways are they similar, and in what ways are they different?

Do alligators and crocodiles come from the same place? Do alligators eat what crocodiles eat?

# Crocodile Facts

Crocodiles can live for 50 to 70 years. They originally come from the Americas, Africa, Asia and Australia, where they live in saltwater and freshwater environments. The color of their scales can be gray, grayish-green, or olive-brown. Their teeth can be seen even when their mouths are closed. Crocodiles can grow between 9 and 20 feet long and weigh up to 2,000 pounds. They like to eat fish, frogs, birds, cattle, and smaller crocodiles.

**Does a crocodile make a good pet? No, it does not!** A crocodile will bite and eat anything that gets close to it, including humans!

# Alligator Facts

Alligators can live for 35 to 50 years. They originally come from the United States and China, where they live in freshwater environments. The color of their scales can be dark gray or black. Their teeth are hidden when their mouths are closed. They can grow between 8 and 15 feet long and weigh up to 1,100 pounds. Alligators like to eat fish, frogs, birds, rodents, deer, snakes, turtles, and even smaller alligators.

**Does an alligator make a good pet? No, it does not!** An alligator may bite you, but unlike some crocodiles, it is less likely to eat you.

Wow! There are many types of crocodiles and alligators from all over the world. Crocodiles can live in both saltwater and freshwater, while alligators reside predominantly in freshwater. They both have similar diets, but crocodiles consider humans as food, whereas alligators do not. Crocodiles have large "fourth" teeth located in their bottom jaws that point upward next to their nostrils. Crocodiles are generally bigger than alligators and can live longer.

## The table below lists the differences between crocodiles and alligators:

|  | Crocodile | Alligator |
|---|---|---|
| Place of Origin | The Americas, Africa, Asia, and Australia | United States and China |
| Habitat | saltwater and freshwater | freshwater |
| Color of Scales | gray, grayish-green, olive-brown | dark gray or black |
| Teeth | teeth visible when mouth is closed | mouth closed teeth not visible |
| Length | 9 to 20 feet (2.7 to 6.1 meters) | 8 to 15 feet (2.4 to 4.6 meters) |
| Weight | up to 2000 pounds (907 kilograms) | up to 1100 pounds (499 kilograms) |
| Food | fish, frogs, birds, rodents, cattle, deer, snails, and smaller crocodiles | fish, frogs, birds, rodents, deer, snakes, turtles, and smaller alligators |
| Lifespan | 50 to 70 years | 35 to 50 years |

# Why is a toad called a toad if it looks like a frog?

Do toads look like frogs?

Which one is a toad, and which one is a frog?

## Do toads *really* look like frogs?

Yes! They both have similar body shapes and sizes, and their eyes are located on their heads in the same way.
As you can see, side by side, they have a similar look.
They can both hop using their hind legs.

## In what other ways are they similar, and in what ways are they different?

Do frogs and toads come from the same place?
Do frogs eat what toads eat?

# Toad Facts

Toads can live for 3 to 10 plus years. They originate from all continents except Antarctica and typically live in fields, grasslands, and forests. Their skin can be green, olive, black, or brown, and is typically dry, bumpy, and warty. Their hind legs are short, so they hop short distances. They like to eat insects and mice, but if food is scarce, they will eat smaller toads.

**Does a toad make a good pet? Yes, it does!** It is small, and you can keep it in a tank appropriate for its size.

# Frog Facts

Frogs can live for 4 to 10 plus years. They originate from all continents except Antarctica and typically live near water bodies like ponds, lakes, and swamps. Their skin can be green, gray, olive, orange, yellow, blue, or purple, and is typically smooth, moist, and slimy. Their hind legs are long, so they hop long distances. They like to eat insects and small fish, but if food is scarce, they will eat smaller frogs.

**Does a frog make a good pet? Yes, it does!** Some species do. You can keep it in a tank appropriate for its size.

Wow! Toads and frogs live on every continent except Antarctica. They have a similar diet of insects and will eat smaller toads and frogs when food is scarce. Toads have bumpy skin with warts and live in drier areas, while frogs have smooth, moist, slimy skin and live near water bodies like lakes, ponds, and swamps. Frogs' hind legs are typically longer than toads' legs. Frogs and toads can be similar in size, and they have similar lifespans.

**The table below lists the differences between toads and frogs:**

|  | Toad | Frog |
|---|---|---|
| **Place of Origin** | Asia, Africa, North America, South America, Europe, Australia | Asia, Africa, North America, South America, Europe, Australia |
| **Habitat** | fields, grasslands, forests | near ponds, lakes, swamps |
| **Color of Skin** | gray, green, olive, black, brown | green, gray, olive, orange, yellow, blue, purple |
| **Texture** | bumpy, dry, and warty | smooth, moist, and slimy |
| **Length** | 1 to 6 inches (2.5 to 15 centimeters) | 1 to 12 inches (2.5 to 30 centimeters) |
| **Weight** | less than an ounce to 3 pounds (less than 1.4 kilograms) | less than an ounce to 6.6 pounds (up to 3 kilograms) |
| **Food** | insects, newts, smaller toads, and mice | insects, small fish, smaller frogs |
| **Lifespan** | 3 to 15 years | 4 to 15 years |

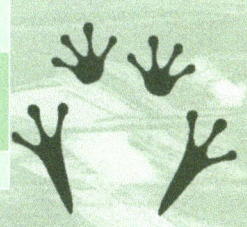

# Why is a porpoise called a porpoise if it looks like a dolphin?

**Do porpoises look like dolphins?**

**Which one is a porpoise, and which one is a dolphin?**

## Do porpoises *really* look like dolphins?

Yes! They both have a similar body shape and fins. As you can see, side by side, they have a similar look. Both animals can leap out of the water and breathe air.

## In what other ways are they similar, and in what ways are they different?

Do porpoises and dolphins come from the same place? Do porpoises eat what dolphins eat?

# Porpoise Facts

Porpoises can live for 8 to 20 years. They inhabit the North Atlantic and North Pacific Oceans, with populations residing in cool coastal waters. Their skin color can be gray or black, with a white underbelly. Porpoises have small body types with blunt snouts, a triangular dorsal fin, and pectoral fins on both sides to help them swim. They can grow up to 6 feet long and weigh up to 200 pounds. Porpoises like to eat fish, octopuses, and squid.

**Do porpoises make good pets? No, they do not!** Porpoises live in the ocean, and you don't! They are shy and do not interact well with humans.

# Dolphin Facts

Dolphins can live for 20 to 50 years. They are found all over the world, including in tropical and temperate oceans, rivers, and cool coastal waters. Their skin color can be gray or pink. Dolphins have large bodies, noticeable snouts, a slightly hooked, triangular-shaped dorsal fin, and pectoral fins on both sides to help them swim. They can grow between 6 and 12 feet long and weigh up to 1,100 pounds. Dolphins eat fish, squid, shrimp, and octopuses.

**Do dolphins make good pets? No, they do not!** Dolphins live in the ocean, and you don't! Although dolphins can be trained to perform shows and are friendly to humans, they require a living space much larger than a backyard pool.

Wow! Both porpoises and dolphins live in coastal waters, but porpoises are usually found in colder waters, whereas dolphins can be found in both cold and tropical waters. They have similar diets. Dolphins are generally larger than porpoises and tend to live much longer. Dolphins can be friendly to humans, while porpoises are typically shy.

**The table below lists the differences between porpoises and dolphins:**

|  | Porpoise | Dolphin |
|---|---|---|
| Place of Origin | they do not originate from a single specific region, but are primarily found in the North Atlantic Ocean, the North Pacific Ocean | they do not originate from a single specific region, but are found all over the world |
| Habitat | cool coastal waters | warm coastal waters, cool coastal waters, rivers |
| Color of Skin | gray, black with white underbelly | gray, pink |
| Body Type | small body, flat snout, triangular fin on the back, and pectoral fins on the left and right sides | large body, large noticeable snout, slightly hooked triangular fin on the back, and pectoral fins on the left and right sides |
| Length | up to 6 feet (1.8 meters) | 6 to 12 feet (1.8 to 3.6 meters) |
| Weight | up to 200 pounds (91 kilograms) | up to 1100 pounds (500 kilograms) |
| Food | fish, octopuses, and squid | fish, squid, shrimp, and octopuses |
| Lifespan | 8 to 20 years | 20 to 50 years |

# Why is an emu called an emu if it looks like an ostrich?

Do emus look like ostriches?
Which one is an emu, and which one is an ostrich?

## Do emus *really* look like ostriches?

Yes! They both have long necks and large round bodies. As you can see, side by side, they look very similar. Both birds can run at high speeds.

## In what other ways are they similar, and in what ways are they different?

Do emus and ostriches come from the same place?
Do emus eat what ostriches eat?

# Emu Facts

Emus can live for up to 30 years. They originally come from Australia, where they live in open plains and tropical woodlands. The color of their feathers can be a mix of brown, gray, and black. They are typically between 4 and 6 feet tall and weigh between 50 and 130 pounds. Emus like to eat seeds, fruits, grass, plants, and insects.

**Do emus make good pets? Maybe!** If you hatch baby emus, they will form a strong attachment to you. However, you must ensure that emus are given a significant amount of space to move and grow. Emus also require the company of other emus for social interaction.

# Ostrich Facts

Ostriches can live for up to 40 years. They originally come from Africa, where they live in places like grasslands and shrublands. The color of their feathers can be black, white, or brown. They are typically between 6 and 9 feet tall and weigh between 220 and 330 pounds. Ostriches like to eat roots, leaves, flowers, seeds, insects, lizards, frogs, and mice.

**Do ostriches make good pets? No, they do not!** Ostriches can be aggressive and territorial.

Wow! Emus are native to Australia, and ostriches are native to Africa, but both animals are now found on farms all over the world. While ostriches and emus eat seeds and insects, their diets do vary. Ostriches are bigger than emus and tend to live longer. Ostriches don't make good pets, but emus are more docile, and given the proper space to move and grow, they can be kept as pets.

The table below lists the differences between emus and ostriches:

|  | Emu | Ostrich |
|---|---|---|
| Place of Origin | Australia | Africa |
| Habitat | open plains, tropical woodlands, grasslands | grasslands, shrublands |
| Color of Feathers | brown, black, gray | black, white, brown |
| Length | 4 to 6 feet (1.2 to 1.8 meters) | 6 to 9 plus feet (1.8 to 2.7 meters) |
| Weight | 50 to 130 pounds (23 to 59 kilograms) | 220 to 330 pounds (100 to 150 kilograms) |
| Food | seeds, fruits, grass, plants, insects | roots, leaves, flowers, seeds, insects, lizards, frogs, and mice |
| Lifespan | up to 30 years | up to 40 years |

# Back to Our Questions!

### Why is a guinea pig called a guinea pig if it looks like a hamster?

Early traders mistakenly thought guinea pigs came from Guinea and named them 'pigs' because of their squealing sounds and round body shape.

### Why is a crocodile called a crocodile if it looks like an alligator?

Crocodile comes from the Greek words *kroke* (meaning pebble or gravel) and *dielos* (worm or man), while alligator comes from the Spanish word *el lagarto* (the lizard). Even though these animals look alike, they were named by different people at different times.

### Why is a toad called a toad if it looks like a frog?

The Old English words "tada" (toad) and "frogga" (frog) were used to distinguish the dry, warty toad from the smooth, slimy frog.

### Why is a porpoise called a porpoise if it looks like a dolphin?

Porpoise got its name from the Latin words *porcus* (pig) and *piscis* (fish) because people thought its round body and short snout looked like a pig. Dolphin, on the other hand, comes from the Greek word *delphís*, meaning 'fish with a womb,' since it is a mammal that gives birth to live young. Even though a porpoise looks like a dolphin, they were given different names because of these differences.

### Why is an emu called an emu if it looks like an ostrich?

Emu comes from the Portuguese word *ema*, meaning large bird, while ostrich comes from the Old French word *ostrice*, which comes from Latin for 'big bird.' Even though they look alike, they were named by different people at different times.

## What Did We Learn?

We learned that many animals look alike but are very different! Some animals come from different countries, but their colors, sizes, and lifespans can be similar, making them difficult to tell apart. They are called by different names because of the people and places where they were discovered. We also learned that some animals that look alike can make good pets, while others do not.

Although we would love to have all these interesting animals as pets, we know this is not possible due to the dangers, locations, and temperaments of these wonderful creatures.

39

# About the Authors

**Donna Defoe's** curiosity about animals began during childhood visits to the local zoo. Now, she enjoys sharing this passion with her family through frequent trips to zoos and aquariums. Donna has always been curious about why certain animals that look alike are called by different names. Her son's insightful question about this mystery inspired her to write this book, aiming to encourage young readers to explore and appreciate the animal kingdom's diversity.

**Dr. Delvin Defoe** has been passionate about writing since his college days, where he honed his skills in crafting short stories and technical articles. His love for storytelling and exploration led him to create this engaging children's book, inspired by his inquisitive "little Einstein," Justin, who is always curious about the wonders of life, animals, and nature. His son's question about why some animals that look alike are called by different names sparked the investigation that culminated in this book.

www.ingramcontent.com/pod-product-compliance
Lightning Source LLC
Chambersburg PA
CBHW040000040426
42337CB00032B/5165